# HANDI

# Cats

Written by

Camille de la Bedoyere

# Miles KeLLY

First published in 2015 by Miles Kelly Publishing Ltd
Harding's Barn, Bardfield End Green, Thaxted, Essex, CM6 3PX, UK

2 4 6 8 10 9 7 5 3 1

Publishing Director  Belinda Gallagher
Creative Director  Jo Cowan
Editorial Director  Rosie Neave
Design Manager  Simon Lee
Image Manager  Liberty Newton
Production Manager  Elizabeth Collins
Reprographics  Stephan Davis, Jennifer Cozens, Thom Allaway

ISBN 978-1-78209-779-2

Printed in China

British Library Cataloguing-in-Publication Data
A catalogue record for this book is available from the British Library

## ACKNOWLEDGEMENTS

All artworks are from the Miles Kelly Artwork Bank.

The publishers would like to thank the following sources for the use of their photographs:

**Alamy** 12 Darren Kirk; 18 Profimedia.CZ a.s; 38 ZUMA Press; 44 Tierfotoagentur/R. Richter; 76 Tierfotoagentur/R. Richter; 90 ZUMA Press **Ardea** 16 Cedric Girard/Biosphoto; 28 Jean-Michel Labat; 34 Jean-Michel Labat; 48 Jean-Michel Labat; 50 Jean-Michel Labat; 66 Jean-Michel Labat; 70 John Daniels **Fotolia.com** 14 arnovdulmen; 54 Callaloo Candcy; 56 eSchmidt; 60 Igors Leonovs; 64 farbkombinat; 82 lwfoto; 94 olena **Glowimages.com** Front cover Wegner, P./Arco Images Gmbh; 20 Wegner, P./Arco Images Gmbh; 22 Arco/P. Wegner; 26 Juniors Bildarchiv; 36 Juniors Bildarchiv; 46 Juniors Bildarchiv; 52 Juniors Bildarchiv; 68 Juniors Bildarchiv; 92 ARCO/Digoit, O. **istockphoto.com** 2 Tami Freed; 40 georgeolsson **Photoshot** 24 Wegner, P.; 80 Juniors Tierbildarchiv; 88 Juniors Tierbildarchiv **Rex Features** 42 Gerard Lacz; 72 A Coppel/Newspix; 74 ZUMA Press; 84 Sipa Press **Shutterstock.com** 2 Tami Freed; 4(t) Graham Taylor, (b) Julie Vader; 5(ct) cath5, (cb) Alberto Pérez Veiga, (b) Anton Gvozdikov; 6(bl) dien, (cb) Sari ONeal, (br) Richard Chaff; 7(tr) Hasloo Group Production Studio, (tl) Roxana Bashyrova, (cl) Goodluz, (cr) tab62; 8(t) Ruth Black, (c) bjonesphotography, (b) Deyan Georgiev; 9(t) Julie Clopper, (c) Grey Carnation; 30 devy; 32 Ivonne Wierink; 58 Dobermaraner; 62 infinityyy; 78 Susan Leggett; 86 Joanna22

Every effort has been made to acknowledge the source and copyright holder of each picture.
Miles Kelly Publishing apologizes for any unintentional errors or omissions.

www.mileskelly.net
info@mileskelly.net

# Contents

**Checklist**: Mark off the cats you have seen in the tick boxes above.

# What is a cat?

**P**et cats, like their wild cousins, have long, lithe bodies that are perfect for running, climbing and hunting. They are known for their curious, playful personalities and independent natures.

## Wild cousins

Cats that live with people are called domestic, or pet, cats. They may be much smaller than their wild cousins but they are similar in many ways. Lions, tigers, cheetahs and other bigger members of the cat family also have round faces, sharp fangs and claws, and long tails, just like pet cats.

Wildcats are a small species of the cat, or felid, family. They look like large Tabby cats and live throughout Europe and Africa.

Most pet cats like exploring outdoors. A cat flap allows them to come and go freely.

## Hunters at home

Pet cats enjoy their home comforts and are happy to be fed, cuddled, loved and given somewhere warm to sleep. However, they are more independent than pet dogs and like to come and go as they please.

# Types of cat

Long ago, the first pet cats were bred from wild cats and they probably all looked similar. Today, there are many different types, or breeds, of cat. They are divided into three main groups.

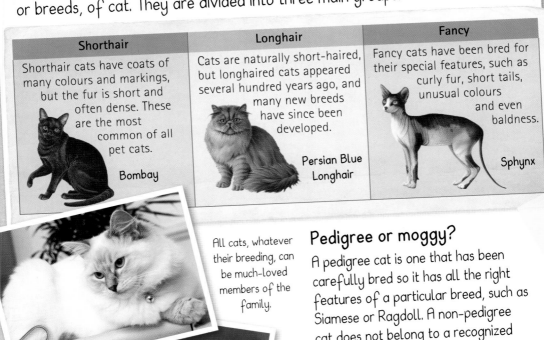

| Shorthair | Longhair | Fancy |
| --- | --- | --- |
| Shorthair cats have coats of many colours and markings, but the fur is short and often dense. These are the most common of all pet cats.<br><br>Bombay | Cats are naturally short-haired, but longhaired cats appeared several hundred years ago, and many new breeds have since been developed.<br><br>Persian Blue Longhair | Fancy cats have been bred for their special features, such as curly fur, short tails, unusual colours and even baldness.<br><br>Sphynx |

All cats, whatever their breeding, can be much-loved members of the family.

## Pedigree or moggy?

A pedigree cat is one that has been carefully bred so it has all the right features of a particular breed, such as Siamese or Ragdoll. A non-pedigree cat does not belong to a recognized breed. Most pet cats are non-pedigree. They are sometimes called 'moggies', and they also make great family pets.

## Competitions

Owners of pedigree cats enjoy showing their cats at competitions, where they are judged on how closely they match the 'ideal' shape, size and colour of their breed. Many cat shows also welcome non-pedigree cats and kittens, which are judged in their own classes.

Longhaired cats are often the stars of a cat show.

# Identifying cats

All cats are similar in size and body shape, unlike dogs. Identifying a breed can often be difficult, but there are key features to look for.

Ears might be pointed or round, set wide or close

Tabby spotted shorthair

Eyes may be round, or almond-shaped

Body could be slender and elegant, or stocky and powerful

Tail may be long, short, fluffy or slender

Face may be wide, or long and thin

Paws may be round or oval, delicate or large

## Coats and markings

Tabbies are striped, Tortoiseshells have patches of red, black and white fur, and Blue cats are smoky blue-grey in colour. Some cats have a thick undercoat that is a different colour to the top coat. Others have two or more colours on a single strand of hair – this is described as 'flecked' or 'ticked'.

Blue

Tabby

Tortoiseshell

# Keeping healthy

In general, cats are healthy animals that may live to the age of 15 or beyond. Keeping a cat in tip-top condition can be simple.

**Food** Cats are meat-eaters and should eat several small meals a day rather than one big meal. They should have clean drinking water available at all times. They should not eat human food, as it can make them sick.

**Exercise** Most cats patrol their territory, or home area, outdoors every day. They also need to play to keep their bodies fit and their reactions fast. However, they also like to sleep a lot, and enjoy many short naps.

**Grooming** Brushing or combing a cat's fur helps to keep it clean and glossy. Grooming a cat also gives the owner a chance to check for fleas, ticks and injuries.

**Visiting the vet** It is important that a cat is seen by a vet regularly so it can have injections against common cat diseases and treatment for pests, such as worms. A vet also advises on diet and general health care. Most pet cats will need to have a simple procedure to stop them from having kittens. This is called neutering.

## Looking out for health issues

A vet can help you identify and treat these common cat problems.

| HEALTH ISSUE | WHAT TO DO |
|---|---|
| Fleas | Fleas are blood-sucking insects that live on cats and their bedding. Cats with fleas often scratch, or suddenly jump and twitch. Cat fleas also bite humans. |
| Bad breath | If a cat has both bad breath and bleeding gums it can be a sign that they have gum disease and sore teeth, which should be treated by a vet. |
| Ear mites | Tiny bugs, called mites, can live in and around a cat's ears, making them very itchy. Mites can also cause ear infections. |
| Sore eyes | Bacterial infections can cause eyes to weep and become sore. This condition is called conjunctivitis. |

# How cats behave

Cats are curious, loving and funny pets. In the course of just a few minutes they can be miaowing for attention, chasing a fly and then washing themselves before curling up and falling asleep with a gentle purr.

## Playing

As soon as kittens are old enough to explore the world they start playing, often leaping on each other with pretend bites. Cats play to practise their hunting skills, but it is also fun, and keeps their minds active. Chasing is a favourite game, cats are fascinated by small things that move fast!

Cats and children make perfect playmates.

## Hunting

It is in a cat's instinct to hunt as all cats are predators. Even cats that have plenty of food at home will hunt. A bell on the cat's collar helps warn other animals that a hunter is nearby. Old cats hunt less.

Cats often bring mice and birds home to eat or play with.

| Indoor | Outdoor |
|---|---|
| Indoor cats are not allowed outside. This lifestyle only suits some breeds. Indoor cats need company and lots of playtime. | It is natural for a cat to want to explore outdoors, and then return home for food and company. This is a balanced lifestyle. |

## Sleeping

Cats need plenty of sleep, just like their wild cousins. Some cats are very active at night, so they sleep all day. Before a cat has a nap it usually spends some time grooming itself with its rough tongue to clean and smooth its fur. Most cats like furry blankets to lie on and sleep in warm places.

A cat can sleep for up to 20 hours a day.

# Mothers and kittens

Some female cats can get pregnant when they are just four months old, so all cats should be neutered by that age if their owner does not want them to have kittens. Females are pregnant for about nine weeks.

## Newborn kittens

When a pregnant cat is ready to give birth she finds a quiet, safe, dark place to have her kittens. As each kitten is born, the mother licks it clean. This licking also encourages the kittens to start breathing. At first, the kittens rely on their mother for everything.

Newborn kittens are blind, deaf and helpless.

Kittens 'knead' their mother's body to make her milk flow.

## Hungry kittens

The mother cat must keep her kittens safe, warm and well-fed. They feed on milk from her body, and mothers often purr when their kittens are suckling. The milk is full of goodness, and the kittens quickly grow. They eat solid food from the age of about 3—4 weeks.

## Caring for kittens

At first, kittens should only be given very small portions of food. By the time they are 6—8 weeks old, most kittens are weaned (they no longer drink their mother's milk). By 9—10 weeks of age they should visit the vet for their first vaccinations.

Newborn kittens are tiny, weak and unable to see or hear properly.

Once kittens are **one week** old their eyes are just opening and their legs can stretch and scrabble.

At **three weeks** kittens look around, listen, and are able to crawl or shuffle.

At **four weeks** old kittens are able to walk and start to pounce and play.

# How to use this book

Cats are much-loved pets that have earned a place in our hearts and homes. By filling in the pages of this book you will learn how to recognize 42 breeds. There are spaces for your notes, sketches and photos.

## Photofile
This photo may show the breed in action, as a kitten, in a different colourway, or a different but related breed, and is accompanied by extra information.

## My observations
Start by writing down the date of your sighting. Then make a note of any colours and markings. Is it an older cat or a kitten? Notice how the cat behaves. Is its playing? Is it eating or miaowing?

## My drawings and photos
Fill these spaces with your sketches and photographs.

## Photos
Take photos of cats that belong to friends and family. Have your camera ready – cats move fast, so you have to be prepared! Natural light will give you the best pictures. Experiment with different angles and see what works best.

## Drawings
Use a soft pencil, such as 2B, because the lead is easy to rub out. Look carefully at the cat's body and head shape. Add arrows with labels such as 'tall, pointed ears' and 'long, fluffy fur'. You don't always need to draw the whole cat – try just sketching the head.

### MY OBSERVATIONS

Date:

Adult or kitten:

Colour of fur:

Colour of eyes:

Special physical features:

Behaviour:

### MY DRAWINGS AND PHOTOS

I saw this cat:   in a house   in a garden

The snub nose of a Persian is desc as 'peke' after the Pekingese bree dog, which also has a flat face. kitten's blue eyes will soon turn the characteristic copper.

## Where?
Tick one of the boxes on the location bar to record where you had your sighting.

60

**Main text**
Every right-hand page has a main paragraph to introduce each breed.

**Colour coding**
The entries in this book are organized into sections. Each section covers breeds belonging to one of three different types of cat. The pages of each section are colour-coded, making it easy to find the breed you have spotted.

# Persian Blue Longhair

Like all Persians, Blues need plenty of attention. They need to be groomed regularly, so their fur doesn't mat or give them furballs. Kittens are usually born with some tabby markings, but this banding gradually fades to a solid blue coat. Persian Blues prefer to be indoors, and like to be fussed over.

SIZE  Medium
EYE COLOUR  Copper or orange
FUR COLOUR  Blue
CHARACTER  Friendly and calm
SPECIAL FEATURE  Orange eyes
COUNTRY OF ORIGIN  Persia

**Fact file**
This box gives you key information about each breed.

Small ears set well apart

Large, round head

Snub nose

Flat face

Solid, stout body

Short, thick tail

**Main illustration**
A large, detailed illustration shows the key features of each breed.

SEEN IT?

in the street ○    at a cat show ○    on TV/in a film ○        61

**Labels**
Around the main illustration, labels point out the most important features, such as head shape, fur length, colours and markings.

**Seen it?**
Once you've seen a particular breed, tick the 'Seen It?' circle.

11

# MY OBSERVATIONS

Date: _____

Adult or kitten: _____

Colour of fur: _____

Colour of eyes: _____

Special physical features: _____

_____

_____

Behaviour: _____

_____

_____

## MY DRAWINGS AND PHOTOS

Burmillas, like this pretty kitten, are a type of Asian Self with silky, silvery fur and elegant bodies. The tips of the hairs should be darker than the roots.

I saw this cat:  in a house  ○   in a garden  ○

# Asian Self

These beautiful cats have large, expressive eyes and they like a lot of attention. They are active, energetic animals that love to play. Asian Selfs can become very attached to their owners, following them around and miaowing until they are stroked or entertained. Very intelligent, Asian Selfs are good at solving problems, such as opening doors. Healthy cats, they can live for 15 years or more.

SIZE  Small-medium

EYE COLOUR  Yellow, gold or green

FUR COLOUR  Various including black, chocolate-brown, smoky-blue, reddish, and cream

CHARACTER  Charming and energetic

SPECIAL FEATURE  Walks on a lead

COUNTRY OF ORIGIN  Various

Long tail, tapers towards the tip

Wide, rounded head

Large, round eyes

Straight back

Blunt muzzle

Strong body

Tabby stripes on legs and tail

SEEN IT?

# MY OBSERVATIONS

Date: _____

Adult or kitten: _____

Colour of fur: _____

Colour of eyes: _____

Special physical features: _____

_____

_____

Behaviour: _____

_____

_____

This is an Asian Leopard Cat. Bengals were bred by mating pet cats with these wild ones. It is about the same size as a pet cat, but it has longer legs.

## MY DRAWINGS AND PHOTOS

I saw this cat:   in a house  ◯   in a garden  ◯

# Bengal

Although independent, Bengals like company. They were bred from a wild Asian cat and a Tabby, so they combine the qualities of both types. They have an athletic body and like to hunt, or take long trips to explore outdoors. Snow Bengals have light-coloured coats with dark markings. Their eyes are blue or blue-green.

**SIZE** Medium-large

**EYE COLOUR** Gold, green, hazel or blue

**FUR COLOUR** Spots and marbling on cream, orangey or brown fur

**CHARACTER** Independent and playful

**SPECIAL FEATURE** Likes water

**COUNTRY OF ORIGIN** USA

Wide face

Tabby-like markings on face

Strong, long body

Large, round paws

Short hind legs

SEEN IT?

# MY OBSERVATIONS

Date: _____

Adult or kitten: _____

Colour of fur: _____

Colour of eyes: _____

Special physical features: _____

_____

_____

Behaviour: _____

_____

_____

Bombay breeders hoped to develop a cat that looked like a black panther. Like panthers, these cats like to sit in high places so they have a good view of everything below them.

# MY DRAWINGS AND PHOTOS

I saw this cat:    in a house  ◯    in a garden  ◯

# Bombay

Originally bred from Burmese cats, Bombays are black Asian Selfs. These sociable animals love company and purr loudly when they are around people. Bombays have a lot of energy — they like to play, and often sharpen their claws on furniture. They can be bossy, so they may not get on well with other cats. However, Bombays have been known to bond with dogs.

**SIZE** Small-medium

**EYE COLOUR** Gold, copper or yellow-green

**FUR COLOUR** Black

**CHARACTER** Sociable and elegant

**SPECIAL FEATURE** Shiny coat

**COUNTRY OF ORIGIN** USA

Large, round eyes

Round, wide head

Long, sleek body

Dense but soft, glossy fur

Long tail with a rounded tip

Small paws with black pads

SEEN IT?

# MY OBSERVATIONS

Date: _____

Adult or kitten: _____

Colour of fur: _____

Colour of eyes: _____

Special physical features: _____

_____

_____

Behaviour: _____

_____

_____

This Bicolour mother cat is about to pick up her kitten. Cats gently hold their young in their mouths, gripping onto the loose skin on the back of a kitten's neck. This doesn't hurt the kitten at all.

## MY DRAWINGS AND PHOTOS

I saw this cat:    in a house ◯    in a garden ◯

# British Bicolour Shorthair

These cats can be recognized by their coat of two colours that form solid patches of fur. Black-and-white Bicolours are popular and are sometimes called Magpie cats. Cream-and-white Bicolours are more unusual. These cats make good family pets because they have lively, friendly personalities. Bicolours are curious, playful and intelligent. They are long-lived cats and can reach the age of 14 or more.

**SIZE**  Medium-large

**EYE COLOUR**  Gold, orange or copper-orange

**FUR COLOUR**  Cream and white, red and white, blue and white, or black and white

**CHARACTER**  Friendly and smart

**SPECIAL FEATURE**  Patched coat

**COUNTRY OF ORIGIN**  Various

Soft, silky, dense fur

Large, round eyes

Strong, agile body

SEEN IT?

Short, thick tail

Fur in patches of two colours

Short legs

Large, rounded paws

# MY OBSERVATIONS

Date: _____

Adult or kitten: _____

Colour of fur: _____

Colour of eyes: _____

Special physical features: _____

_____

_____

Behaviour: _____

_____

_____

This mother and her kitten are British Bicolour Shorthairs, which means their fur is two colours (blue and white). The kitten was born with blue eyes, but they will eventually change colour to gold.

## MY DRAWINGS AND PHOTOS

I saw this cat:  in a house ◯  in a garden ◯

# British Blue Shorthair

These fluffy cats may be described as shorthaired, but their coats are as dense and soft as the coats of many longhaired breeds. Despite having strong, muscled bodies, Blue Shorthairs are not very energetic. They enjoy exercise, but are very happy to stay indoors and settle somewhere warm. These cats enjoy company.

**SIZE** Medium-large

**EYE COLOUR** Gold

**FUR COLOUR** Blue-grey

**CHARACTER** Loving and easy-going

**SPECIAL FEATURE** Very soft fur

**COUNTRY OF ORIGIN** Various

Round eyes

Snub nose with a blue nose pad

Large cheek pads give the cat a 'smiley' face

Stocky, muscular body

Short legs

Round paws with blue pads

SEEN IT?

# MY OBSERVATIONS

Date: _____

Adult or kitten: _____

Colour of fur: _____

Colour of eyes: _____

Special physical features: _____

_____

_____

Behaviour: _____

_____

_____

This British Tortoiseshell's fur is described as 'lilac tortoiseshell-and-white'. Often known as 'Torties', Tortoiseshell cats usually have a stocky build and large orange or copper eyes.

## MY DRAWINGS AND PHOTOS

I saw this cat:   in a house  ◯   in a garden  ◯

# British Tortoiseshell Shorthair

Almost all Tortoiseshell Shorthairs are female. Their unusual markings are linked to being female, so few males are born — those that are born are unlikely to be able to father kittens. They can vary in appearance and personality. They are affectionate, intelligent and good-natured.

**SIZE** Medium-large

**EYE COLOUR** Orange or copper

**FUR COLOUR** Patches of red, black and white, or cream

**CHARACTER** Clever and friendly

**SPECIAL FEATURE** Unusual colours

**COUNTRY OF ORIGIN** Various

Round eyes

Wide head

Strong, stocky body

Thick tail

Short legs

Large, round paws

SEEN IT?

in the street ◯    at a cat show ◯    on TV/in a film ◯

23

# MY OBSERVATIONS

Date:

Adult or kitten:

Colour of fur:

Colour of eyes:

Special physical features:

Behaviour:

British Shorthairs have thick fur, which may have arisen after street cats were bred with Persians. They tend to be healthy cats and are often compared to cuddly teddy bears!

## MY DRAWINGS AND PHOTOS

I saw this cat:    in a house ◯    in a garden ◯

# British White Shorthair

With a pure white coat, White Shorthairs occasionally have different-coloured eyes — one blue and one gold or copper. They are heavy, well-built cats with short legs and tails. Blue-eyed cats often have hearing problems. White Shorthairs are gentle, friendly cats that are happy to be around children and like a quiet life indoors. These cats enjoy their food, and can become overweight if fed too much.

**SIZE** Medium-large

**EYE COLOUR** Blue, gold or copper

**FUR COLOUR** White

**CHARACTER** Charming and friendly

**SPECIAL FEATURE** Odd-coloured eyes

**COUNTRY OF ORIGIN** Various

Ears are set well apart

Eyes are sometimes different colours

Large, bulky body

Thick fur

Short legs

Short tail

Large, round paws

SEEN IT?

in the street ◯　　at a cat show ◯　　on TV/in a film ◯

# MY OBSERVATIONS

Date:

Adult or kitten:

Colour of fur:

Colour of eyes:

Special physical features:

Behaviour:

A mother cat is called a queen. She can give birth to kittens of different colours within one litter, such as these two Burmese youngsters, one chocolate (left) and the other red.

# MY DRAWINGS AND PHOTOS

I saw this cat:   in a house ○   in a garden ○

# Burmese

Full of character, Burmese like to be the centre of attention and enjoy being with people. Burmese can get lonely if they have to spend whole days without company. They are very clever, and can be trained to fetch small things. Burmese tend to be very healthy and can live for up to 20 years.

**SIZE** Small-medium

**EYE COLOUR** Yellow or gold

**FUR COLOUR** Various solid colours including black, brown, blue, red and cream

**CHARACTER** Tough and sociable

**SPECIAL FEATURE** Long-lived

**COUNTRY OF ORIGIN** Burma

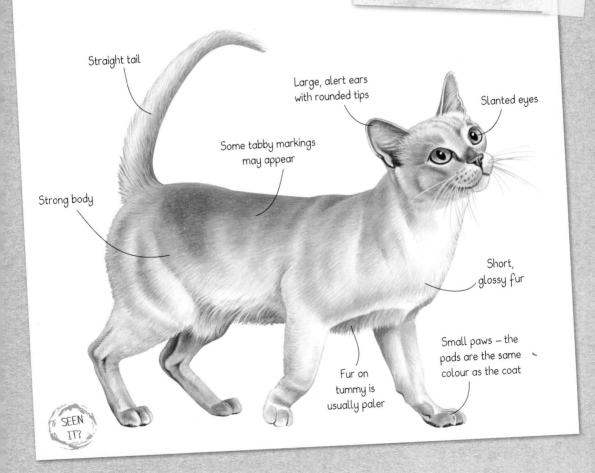

Straight tail

Large, alert ears with rounded tips

Slanted eyes

Some tabby markings may appear

Strong body

Short, glossy fur

Fur on tummy is usually paler

Small paws – the pads are the same colour as the coat

SEEN IT?

# MY OBSERVATIONS

Date: _____

Adult or kitten: _____

Colour of fur: _____

Colour of eyes: _____

Special physical features: _____

_____

_____

Behaviour: _____

_____

_____

This agile leaper is a Devon Rex, a breed that has been developed from the Cornish Rex. The Devon Rex has a slightly coarser coat and a broader chest than its Cornish cousin.

## MY DRAWINGS AND PHOTOS

I saw this cat:   in a house ◯   in a garden ◯

# Cornish Rex

Peculiar-looking, Cornish Rexes have soft, wavy fur. These cats love to play and need lots of attention to keep them entertained. They are naturally curious, clever and good-natured. Cornish Rexes need to be groomed at least once a week to keep their fur in good condition.

**SIZE** Small-medium

**EYE COLOUR** Any

**FUR COLOUR** Any colour and any markings

**CHARACTER** Playful and sociable

**SPECIAL FEATURE** Wavy coat

**COUNTRY OF ORIGIN** UK

Small face with playful expression

Long nose

Slender, dainty body

Long, thin tail

Wavy, plush fur

SEEN IT?

in the street ○     at a cat show ○     on TV/in a film ○

# MY OBSERVATIONS

Date: _____

Adult or kitten: _____

Colour of fur: _____

Colour of eyes: _____

Special physical features:

_____

_____

Behaviour: _____

_____

_____

As this young Egyptian Mau stretches out, its long toes are clearly visible. Unlike dogs, cats have curved claws that can be retracted (pulled back and tucked away).

## MY DRAWINGS AND PHOTOS

I saw this cat:   in a house ◯   in a garden ◯

# Egyptian Mau

Originally from Egypt, these cats are thought to be related to cats honoured by the ancient Egyptians. They are the only spotted breed of cats, although they also have many striped markings. Egyptian Maus are very active, and they love attention. They are one of the few cats that can be walked on a lead.

**SIZE** Medium

**EYE COLOUR** Light green

**FUR COLOUR** Brown or black markings on silver, blue or black fur

**CHARACTER** Clever and active

**SPECIAL FEATURE** Can be walked on a lead

**COUNTRY OF ORIGIN** Egypt and USA

'M' marking on forehead

Wide-set ears

Almond-shaped eyes

Short nose

Dark stripe down spine

Dark flecks and spotted markings

Elegant, athletic body

SEEN IT?

in the street ◯    at a cat show ◯    on TV/in a film ◯

# MY OBSERVATIONS

Date: _____

Adult or kitten: _____

Colour of fur: _____

Colour of eyes: _____

Special physical features: _____

_____

_____

Behaviour: _____

_____

_____

The Havana face is unique amongst cat breeds, with a long, slender nose, high cheekbones and enormous ears. Havanas don't like the cold, so they will bask in sunshine whenever they can.

## MY DRAWINGS AND PHOTOS

I saw this cat:     in a house  ◯     in a garden  ◯

# Havana

Elegant Havanas look like Siamese, the breed from which they were bred. Attention-seeking cats, Havanas like to be around people, and are especially affectionate. They often play with small objects, and may raise a paw and stare at their owners when they are being ignored. Havanas are graceful, with glossy coats and dainty, slender legs.

SIZE  Medium

EYE COLOUR  Green

FUR COLOUR  Deep brown

CHARACTER  Sociable and intelligent

SPECIAL FEATURE  Long face

COUNTRY OF ORIGIN  Britain and USA

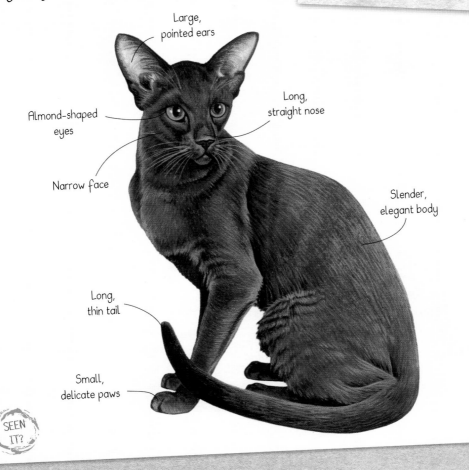

Large, pointed ears

Almond-shaped eyes

Narrow face

Long, straight nose

Slender, elegant body

Long, thin tail

Small, delicate paws

SEEN IT?

# MY OBSERVATIONS

Date: _____

Adult or kitten: _____

Colour of fur: _____

Colour of eyes: _____

Special physical features: _____

_____

_____

Behaviour: _____

_____

_____

When this Korat mother holds her kitten by the scruff of its neck the kitten's body becomes floppy and still. This keeps it safe while the mother moves it.

# MY DRAWINGS AND PHOTOS

I saw this cat:   in a house  ◯    in a garden  ◯

# Korat

One of the oldest breeds, Korats originally came from Thailand. They have a bright, alert expression and enjoy playing. Kittens sometimes have amber eyes, which turn green as they get older. Korats look similar to Russian Blues, but their eyes are paler green in colour. These cats have a thin coat, so they prefer to stay indoors during cold weather.

**SIZE** Medium

**EYE COLOUR** Light green

**FUR COLOUR** Blue-grey with silvery ends

**CHARACTER** Playful and sweet-natured

**SPECIAL FEATURE** Eyes are an unusual shade of green

**COUNTRY OF ORIGIN** Thailand

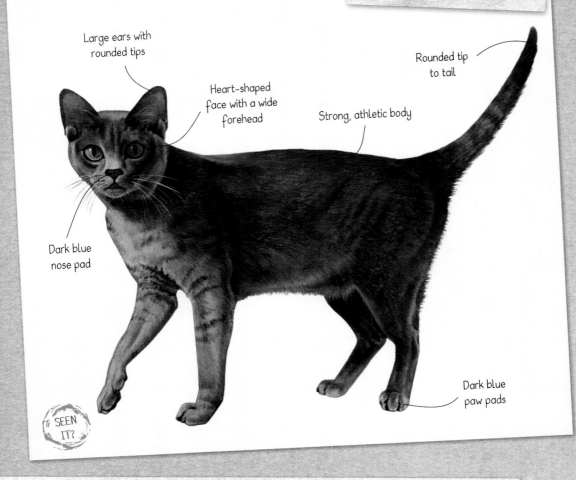

Large ears with rounded tips

Heart-shaped face with a wide forehead

Strong, athletic body

Rounded tip to tail

Dark blue nose pad

Dark blue paw pads

SEEN IT?

in the street ○    at a cat show ○    on TV/in a film ○

# MY OBSERVATIONS

Date: _____

Adult or kitten: _____

Colour of fur: _____

Colour of eyes: _____

Special physical features: _____

_____

Behaviour: _____

_____

_____

At first glance a Russian Blue looks similar to a British Blue, but its body is daintier and its fur has a distinctive sheen. The wide ears are set far apart on the cat's head.

# MY DRAWINGS AND PHOTOS

I saw this cat:   in a house ◯   in a garden ◯

# Russian Blue

Quiet cats, Russian Blues are shy and elegant. However, they are also playful and can even be taken outdoors on a lead. They like children and other animals as long as they can escape for some peace and quiet. Russian Blues can become very attached to their owners. Their fur is extremely dense and soft, and they like being groomed.

SIZE  Medium-large

EYE COLOUR  Bright green

FUR COLOUR  Blue

CHARACTER  Home-loving and friendly

SPECIAL FEATURE  Can be walked on a lead

COUNTRY OF ORIGIN  Russia

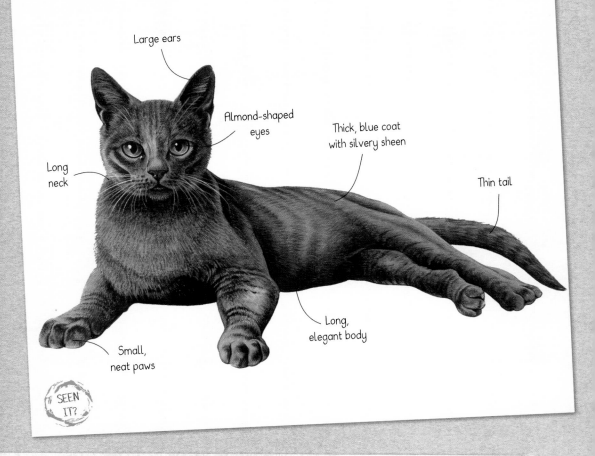

Large ears

Almond-shaped eyes

Thick, blue coat with silvery sheen

Long neck

Thin tail

Small, neat paws

Long, elegant body

SEEN IT?

# MY OBSERVATIONS

Date: _____

Adult or kitten: _____

Colour of fur: _____

Colour of eyes: _____

Special physical features: _____

_____

_____

Behaviour: _____

_____

_____

Savannah cats are not just large – they are huge, like their wild ancestors. These cats are often said to have dog-like personalities and can be taken for a walk on a lead!

# MY DRAWINGS AND PHOTOS

I saw this cat:    in a house ◯    in a garden ◯

# Savannah

These cats were originally bred by crossing Shorthairs with Servals, which are wild African cats. They were therefore named after African grasslands, called savannahs. It is a new breed, which has been developed since the 1980s. Savannahs can be a range of colours, and they are playful, intelligent and sociable in nature.

SIZE  Large

EYE COLOUR  Yellow, gold, green or brown

FUR COLOUR  Brown, black or cream with tabby markings

CHARACTER  Active and feisty

SPECIAL FEATURE  Likes playing with water

COUNTRY OF ORIGIN   USA

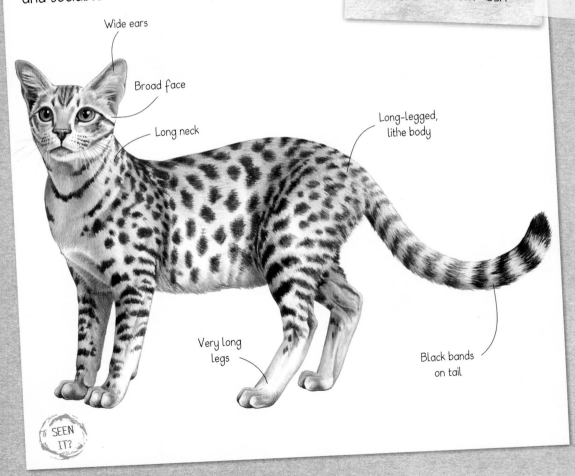

Wide ears

Broad face

Long neck

Long-legged, lithe body

Very long legs

Black bands on tail

SEEN IT?

# MY OBSERVATIONS

Date: _____

Adult or kitten: _____

Colour of fur: _____

Colour of eyes: _____

Special physical features: _____

_____

_____

Behaviour: _____

_____

_____

With their athletic bodies and fast reactions it is no wonder Siamese cats often disappear at night to search for animals to chase. In the day, they are usually content to play with toys.

## MY DRAWINGS AND PHOTOS

I saw this cat:   in a house ◯   in a garden ◯

# Siamese

Distinctive in both looks and personality, Siamese are quite demanding, but they reward their owners with great loyalty and affection. Siamese expect a lot of attention and they will often cry and yowl until they receive it. They are clever and playful, as well as being skilled hunters.

SIZE  Medium

EYE COLOUR  Blue

FUR COLOUR  Shades of cream with darker points

CHARACTER  Bold and clever

SPECIAL FEATURE  Cries rather than miaows

COUNTRY OF ORIGIN  Thailand

Face, ears, legs and tail are darker seal, lilac, chocolate or blue

Thin, dainty body

Almond-shaped eyes

Slender tail

Long, thin legs

Elegant paws

SEEN IT?

# MY OBSERVATIONS

Date: _____

Adult or kitten: _____

Colour of fur: _____

Colour of eyes: _____

Special physical features: _____

_____

_____

Behaviour: _____

_____

_____

Like many cats, Singapuras love to climb trees. However, they often find it harder to come down because their curved claws make a descent more difficult.

# MY DRAWINGS AND PHOTOS

I saw this cat:    in a house ◯    in a garden ◯

# Singapura

The dense but fine coat of the Singapura is soft. The fur is pale cream in colour on the stomach, chest and chin and flecked with darker, richer colours elsewhere. These cats have a particular liking for high places, and often sit at the top of posts or fences to watch what goes on below. They love attention and playing.

**SIZE** Small

**EYE COLOUR** Yellow, green or brown

**FUR COLOUR** Dark gold to cream with darker flecks

**CHARACTER** Mischievous and friendly

**SPECIAL FEATURE** Small and light

**COUNTRY OF ORIGIN** Unknown

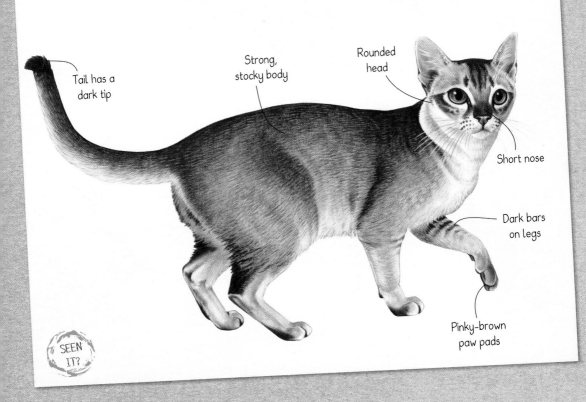

Tail has a dark tip

Strong, stocky body

Rounded head

Short nose

Dark bars on legs

Pinky-brown paw pads

SEEN IT?

## MY OBSERVATIONS

Date: _____

Adult or kitten: _____

Colour of fur: _____

Colour of eyes: _____

Special physical features: _____

_____

_____

Behaviour: _____

_____

_____

Like other cats, grooming is an essential part of a Snowshoe cat's daily routine. Cats use their teeth and rasping tongues to clean every part of their fur, keeping it smooth and glossy.

## MY DRAWINGS AND PHOTOS

I saw this cat:    in a house ◯    in a garden ◯

# Snowshoe

Named after their four white paws, Snowshoes are bred from Siamese and American Shorthairs. The kittens are white when they are born, but gradually darken and may have a range of markings. These cats need to be kept busy and enjoy company. Unusually, Snowshoes like water and have been known to swim.

**SIZE** Medium

**EYE COLOUR** Blue

**FUR COLOUR** Various but mostly blue, seal or chocolate

**CHARACTER** Playful and energetic

**SPECIAL FEATURE** Likes being around water

**COUNTRY OF ORIGIN** USA

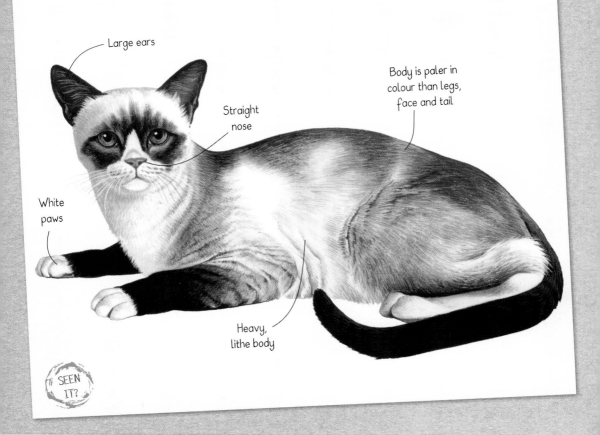

Large ears

Straight nose

Body is paler in colour than legs, face and tail

White paws

Heavy, lithe body

SEEN IT?

## MY OBSERVATIONS

Date: _____

Adult or kitten: _____

Colour of fur: _____

Colour of eyes: _____

Special physical features: _____

_____

Behaviour: _____

_____

_____

This Tabby has the classic pattern, with a dark 'bull's eye' on each flank (side of the body). Both types of Tabby pattern have a clear 'M' marking above the nose.

## MY DRAWINGS AND PHOTOS

I saw this cat:   in a house ◯   in a garden ◯

# Tabby Shorthair

A popular breed, Tabby Shorthairs have existed for a long time. Their coats come in two main patterns — classic and mackerel (which is more striped than the classic variety). Tabbies usually have strong characters, and males especially can be quite independent.

**SIZE** Medium-large

**EYE COLOUR** Gold, copper, green or hazel

**FUR COLOUR** Cream to brown with dark markings

**CHARACTER** Independent and intelligent

**SPECIAL FEATURE** Tabby markings

**COUNTRY OF ORIGIN** Various

Short, wide tail

Strong, athletic body

Large, round eyes

Ears with rounded tips

Short, strong legs

Large, round paws

SEEN IT?

## MY OBSERVATIONS

Date: 10·4·23

Adult or kitten: Kitten

Colour of fur: white & black

Colour of eyes: Brown

Special physical features: white on tail brown nose

Behaviour: Jumpy & exited

## MY DRAWINGS AND PHOTOS

I saw this cat:   in a house ○   in a garden ○

# Tabby Spotted Shorthair

Spotted Shorthairs are similar to other shorthaired Tabbies, but their dark markings are broken up into spots. They usually have a pale, silvery coat, which is dense and soft. Other colours such as blue and chocolate also exist. Spotted Shorthairs are strong, agile cats and they enjoy being outdoors, hunting and exploring. Their legs are quite short and well-muscled.

**SIZE** Medium-large

**EYE COLOUR** Yellow-green, green or hazel

**FUR COLOUR** Silver-grey with dark markings

**CHARACTER** Gentle and good-natured

**SPECIAL FEATURE** Spotted coat

**COUNTRY OF ORIGIN** Various

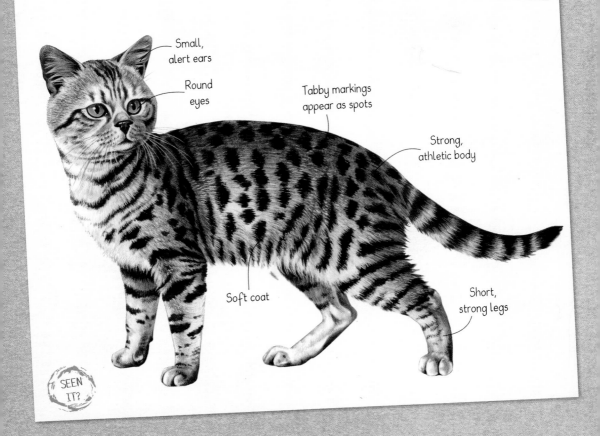

Small, alert ears

Round eyes

Tabby markings appear as spots

Strong, athletic body

Soft coat

Short, strong legs

SEEN IT?

# MY OBSERVATIONS

Date: _____

Adult or kitten: _____

Colour of fur: _____

Colour of eyes: _____

Special physical features: _____

_____

_____

Behaviour: _____

_____

_____

The 'points' (face, paws, tail tip) of some Tonkinese cats are darker than the coat, because of this breed's Siamese roots. Kittens normally have pale points that darken as they mature.

# MY DRAWINGS AND PHOTOS

I saw this cat:   in a house ◯   in a garden ◯

# Tonkinese

Bred from Siamese or Burmese, Tonkinese are also known as 'Tonks' and 'Golden Siamese'. These good-natured cats are quite nosy, and like to be involved in anything that is happening. Tonkinese enjoy exploring outside, but they are happiest when around people. They are quite vocal, and need plenty of activity to keep them entertained.

**SIZE** Medium

**EYE COLOUR** Blue or blue-green

**FUR COLOUR** Various, including cream, blue and dark brown, often with tabby markings

**CHARACTER** Friendly and curious

**SPECIAL FEATURE** Loves running and jumping

**COUNTRY OF ORIGIN** USA

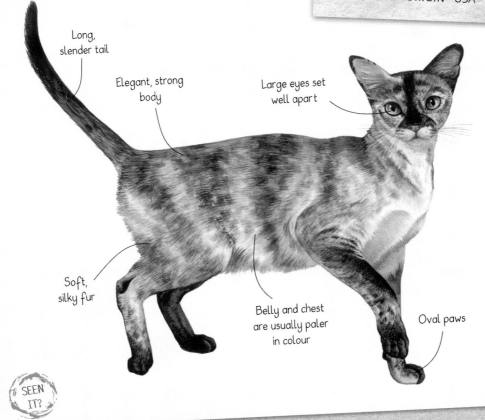

Long, slender tail

Elegant, strong body

Large eyes set well apart

Soft, silky fur

Belly and chest are usually paler in colour

Oval paws

SEEN IT?

# MY OBSERVATIONS

Date: _____

Adult or kitten: _____

Colour of fur: _____

Colour of eyes: _____

Special physical features: _____

_____

_____

Behaviour: _____

_____

_____

Originally, these cats were bred to be pure white but now breeders are developing different colour varieties. Angora Longhairs carry their tails high, often curved over their backs.

# MY DRAWINGS AND PHOTOS

I saw this cat:     in a house ◯     in a garden ◯

# Angora Longhair

These cats have soft, silky fur, without a dense, woolly undercoat. This makes them especially sleek and easy to care for. They were originally bred from Siamese, which gives them long, slender bodies. They love attention and 'talking' to their owners, and are playful, curious cats. The Angora Longhair is also known as the British Angora.

**SIZE** Medium

**EYE COLOUR** Blue or green

**FUR COLOUR** Various, from cream to black with various markings

**CHARACTER** Curious and chatty

**SPECIAL FEATURE** Fine, silky coat

**COUNTRY OF ORIGIN** Turkey

Fur may be one solid colour, flecked or tipped with other colours, or with tabby markings

Ears are wide at base

Slanted eyes

Wide, fluffy tail

Long, thin neck

Long, sleek body

SEEN IT?

# MY OBSERVATIONS

Date:

Adult or kitten:

Colour of fur:

Colour of eyes:

Special physical features:




Behaviour:




The areas of white fur on a Birman's paws are called 'gloves' and the shape of the gloves should match and ideally be symmetrical. The darker areas appear as kittens mature.

## MY DRAWINGS AND PHOTOS

I saw this cat:     in a house ◯     in a garden ◯

# Birman

With bright blue eyes, a pale coat and dark points, Birmans look like longhaired Siamese. The points can be lilac, chocolate, seal or blue, but their paws are always white. Their thick coats are not as dense as the coats of some other Longhairs, but they still need to be regularly brushed. These sweet cats have a loving, quiet character and a soft voice.

SIZE  Medium

EYE COLOUR  Blue

FUR COLOUR  Cream or beige with darker points

CHARACTER  Gentle and loving

SPECIAL FEATURE  White feet

COUNTRY OF ORIGIN  Burma

Round, wide head

Silky fur

Long, heavy body

Dark points, except for paws

White paws

SEEN IT?

Fluffy tail

# MY OBSERVATIONS

Date: _____

Adult or kitten: _____

Colour of fur: _____

Colour of eyes: _____

Special physical features: _____

_____

_____

Behaviour: _____

_____

_____

Cymrics have longer fur on their breeches (legs) and bellies, and around their throats – the fur in this area is called a 'ruff'. These cats sometimes have problems with their spines.

## MY DRAWINGS AND PHOTOS

I saw this cat:     in a house ◯     in a garden ◯

# Cymric

These cats are easily recognized because they don't have a tail. Cymrics are bred from Manxes, although it is hard to breed truly tail-less Cymrics. Depending on the length of their tails, these cats are called Risers, Stumpies, Stubbies or Longies. Cymrics have a good nature, and love to jump up to high places. They are also known as Longhaired Manxes.

SIZE  Medium

EYE COLOUR  Any

FUR COLOUR  Any colour or pattern

CHARACTER  Fun-loving and intelligent

SPECIAL FEATURE  Tail-less

COUNTRY OF ORIGIN  Isle of Man, UK

Medium-sized ears

Broad, round head

Heavy, muscular body

No tail

Large paws

SEEN IT?

# MY OBSERVATIONS

Date: _____

Adult or kitten: _____

Colour of fur: _____

Colour of eyes: _____

Special physical features: _____

_____

_____

Behaviour: _____

_____

_____

Although Maine Coons are hardy cats that love exploring and hunting, they are also known for their friendliness. They enjoy being groomed to keep their thick fur in good condition.

# MY DRAWINGS AND PHOTOS

I saw this cat:     in a house ◯     in a garden ◯

# Maine Coon

An old breed from the USA, Maine Coons have developed thick coats to cope with cold weather. Their coats can be of many colours and patterns, and tabby markings are common. Maine Coons are affectionate cats, but they love the outdoors and need plenty of space to explore, hunt and play. They are known for finding unusual places to curl up and sleep, and often sleep outside.

SIZE  Large

EYE COLOUR  Blue, copper, gold or green

FUR COLOUR  Various colours and markings

CHARACTER  Friendly and playful

SPECIAL FEATURE  Loves the outdoors

COUNTRY OF ORIGIN  USA

Tall ears with pointed tips

Long back

Strong, sturdy body

Silky top coat and dense undercoat

Large, powerful legs

Fluffy tail tip

SEEN IT?

# MY OBSERVATIONS

Date: _____

Adult or kitten: _____

Colour of fur: _____

Colour of eyes: _____

Special physical features: _____

_____

_____

Behaviour: _____

_____

_____

The snub nose of a Persian is described as 'peke' after the Pekingese breed of dog, which also has a flat face. This kitten's blue eyes will soon turn to the characteristic copper.

## MY DRAWINGS AND PHOTOS

I saw this cat:   in a house ◯   in a garden ◯

# Persian Blue Longhair

Like all Persians, Blues need plenty of attention. They need to be groomed regularly, so their fur doesn't mat or give them furballs. Kittens are usually born with some tabby markings, but this banding gradually fades to a solid blue coat. Persian Blues prefer to be indoors, and like to be fussed over.

**SIZE** Medium

**EYE COLOUR** Copper or orange

**FUR COLOUR** Blue

**CHARACTER** Friendly and calm

**SPECIAL FEATURE** Orange eyes

**COUNTRY OF ORIGIN** Persia

Small ears set well apart

Large, round head

Flat face

Snub nose

Solid, stout body

Short, thick tail

SEEN IT?

in the street ◯    at a cat show ◯    on TV/in a film ◯

# MY OBSERVATIONS

Date:

Adult or kitten:

Colour of fur:

Colour of eyes:

Special physical features:

Behaviour:

Red Persian Tabbies are particularly beautiful because their fur colour complements their copper eyes. Persians have short, stocky legs to support their bulky bodies.

# MY DRAWINGS AND PHOTOS

I saw this cat:   in a house ◯   in a garden ◯

# Persian Tabby Longhair

With similar markings to their shorthaired cousins, Tabby Longhairs have dense, long fur. Their coats are silky and require plenty of grooming to keep them knot-free and glossy. Base colours include brown, red or silver, but the tabby markings can vary both in colour and pattern. Mackerel Tabby Longhairs are especially striped. These cats are home-loving animals that like company.

**SIZE** Medium

**EYE COLOUR** Various

**FUR COLOUR** Various base colours with tabby markings

**CHARACTER** Gentle and friendly

**SPECIAL FEATURE** Dense fur

**COUNTRY OF ORIGIN** Persia

Small ears with rounded tips

Wide head

Short snub nose

Solid, well-built body

Short, thick legs

Large, round paws

SEEN IT?

# MY OBSERVATIONS

Date: _____

Adult or kitten: _____

Colour of fur: _____

Colour of eyes: _____

Special physical features: _____

_____

Behaviour: _____

_____

_____

This is a Tortoiseshell Persian – it lacks the white patches of a Tortie-and-White and is a popular colourway for the breed. The fur gets matted easily, especially if the cats play outside.

## MY DRAWINGS AND PHOTOS

I saw this cat:     in a house ◯     in a garden ◯

# Persian Tortoiseshell-and-White Longhair

With splashes of colour and long, fluffy fur, these cats are easy to recognize. Tortoiseshell-and-White Longhairs are members of the Persian family, but with the characteristic red and black blotches of a Tortoiseshell. Like other Tortoiseshells, these cats are all female. They are popular pets because they are not only attractive to look at, but have a gentle, affectionate nature.

SIZE  Medium

EYE COLOUR  Various

FUR COLOUR  Various base colours with tabby markings

CHARACTER  Gentle and friendly

SPECIAL FEATURE  Dense fur

COUNTRY OF ORIGIN  Persia

Broad, solid body

Large, round eyes

Broad face

Bushy tail

Snub nose

Large, round paws

SEEN IT?

## MY OBSERVATIONS

Date: _____

Adult or kitten: _____

Colour of fur: _____

Colour of eyes: _____

Special physical features: _____

_____

_____

Behaviour: _____

_____

_____

Persian Chinchillas – like this kitten – have pale fur that has darker tips. Those with white fur are called Silver Chinchillas and those with cream to apricot fur are Golden Chinchillas.

## MY DRAWINGS AND PHOTOS

I saw this cat:   in a house ◯    in a garden ◯

# Persian White Longhair

Popular cats, Persian White Longhairs have bright eyes and dense, white fur. They are often bred for competitions, and were first developed by crossing Angoras with Persians. Persian Whites like to be groomed – by themselves or their owners. They should be brushed daily to prevent their fur from becoming knotted. These cats are friendly but not very active, and are happy to spend lots of time indoors.

**SIZE** Medium

**EYE COLOUR** Blue, copper or gold

**FUR COLOUR** White

**CHARACTER** Placid and easy-going

**SPECIAL FEATURE** Snow-white coat

**COUNTRY OF ORIGIN** Persia

Snub nose

Small ears set well apart

Stocky, solid body

Thick, fluffy tail

Flat face

Large, round paws

Short, stocky legs

SEEN IT?

in the street ◯    at a cat show ◯    on TV/in a film ◯

# MY OBSERVATIONS

Date: _____

Adult or kitten: _____

Colour of fur: _____

Colour of eyes: _____

Special physical features: _____

_____

_____

Behaviour: _____

_____

_____

## MY DRAWINGS AND PHOTOS

This colourway is described as 'fawn'. Tabby stripes are clearly visible on this cat's front legs. Somalis usually have tufts of fur growing between their toes.

# Somali

Fluffy Somali cats combine the elegance of Abyssinian cats with the long hair of Persians. The fur on their chest, tail and britches (backs of legs) is especially long. There are many coat colours, but each individual hair can have up to ten bands of different shades. Ruddy orange, apricot and warm copper Somalis are most common. These shy cats are active and like to explore, play and hunt outdoors.

**SIZE** Medium

**EYE COLOUR** Green, amber or hazel

**FUR COLOUR** Various, including gold/brown, fawn and cream

**CHARACTER** Active and independent

**SPECIAL FEATURE** Athletic

**COUNTRY OF ORIGIN** USA

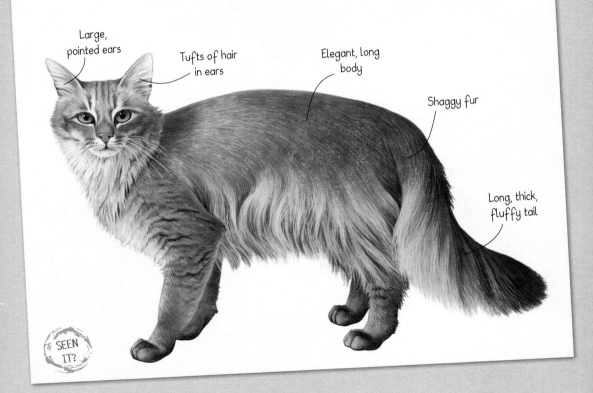

Large, pointed ears

Tufts of hair in ears

Elegant, long body

Shaggy fur

Long, thick, fluffy tail

SEEN IT?

in the street ◯   at a cat show ◯   on TV/in a film ◯

# MY OBSERVATIONS

Date: _____

Adult or kitten: _____

Colour of fur: _____

Colour of eyes: _____

Special physical features: _____

_____

_____

Behaviour: _____

_____

_____

These cats have fluffy fur around their face and neck (where it is called a 'ruff'). The long hair extends onto the chest. These are Asian cats, so they have elegant faces and bodies.

# MY DRAWINGS AND PHOTOS

I saw this cat:     in a house  ◯     in a garden  ◯

# Tiffanie

These cats are Asian Longhairs that are descended from Burmese and Persian Chinchillas. Their hair is not as long as other Longhairs, although it still needs regular brushing to remain soft and silky. Tiffanies are extremely affectionate cats that follow their owners, calling for food or attention. They are known for their intelligence, and love to play with toys and people.

**SIZE** Medium

**EYE COLOUR** Yellow, gold or green

**FUR COLOUR** Various

**CHARACTER** Affectionate and intelligent

**SPECIAL FEATURE** Coat is pale cream in kittens, and darker in adults

**COUNTRY OF ORIGIN** Persia

Ears are set well apart

Wide-set eyes

Round chin

Elegant, muscular body

Long, fluffy tail

Slim legs

SEEN IT?

## MY OBSERVATIONS

Date: _____

Adult or kitten: _____

Colour of fur: _____

Colour of eyes: _____

Special physical features: _____

_____

_____

Behaviour: _____

_____

_____

Most cats are known for their dislike of water and can even be fussy about how they are served their drinking water. Turkish Vans don't mind getting wet, and even play with water.

## MY DRAWINGS AND PHOTOS

I saw this cat:   in a house ◯   in a garden ◯

# Turkish Van

These cats originally developed in an area around Lake Van, in Turkey. Unusually, they like water and are also known as 'Turkish swimming cats'. Their silky fur is long but without a thick undercoat, so it is glossy and soft, and does not knot as easily as other longhaired cats. They are active and intelligent cats that like to play.

SIZE  Large

EYE COLOUR  Amber or blue

FUR COLOUR  White with some markings

CHARACTER  Active and lively

SPECIAL FEATURE  Likes swimming

COUNTRY OF ORIGIN  Turkey

Large ears

Long, strong body

Markings on tail, head and base of ears

Broad chest

Long, muscular legs

Tufted tail

SEEN IT?

in the street ○    at a cat show ○    on TV/in a film ○

# MY OBSERVATIONS

Date: _____

Adult or kitten: _____

Colour of fur: _____

Colour of eyes: _____

Special physical features: _____

_____

_____

Behaviour: _____

_____

_____

An American Curl being judged at a cat show. Curls are known as people-cats as they love attention but don't demand it. They like to nuzzle up to their owners' faces. Curls can be trained to 'fetch'.

# MY DRAWINGS AND PHOTOS

I saw this cat:   in a house ◯   in a garden ◯

# American Curl

These unusual-looking cats are descended from a single female, called Shulasmith. Her ears curled backwards. Kittens start life with normal ears, which curl over time. American Curls are good-natured cats. They love to play, even as they get older. These cats are loving and relish lots of attention.

SIZE  Medium

EYE COLOUR  All colours

FUR COLOUR  All colours and patterns

CHARACTER  Loyal and friendly

SPECIAL FEATURE  Curled ears

COUNTRY OF ORIGIN  USA

Ears are fully curled after 4 to 5 months

Slender, well-proportioned body

Silky coat

Fluffy tail

SEEN IT?

# MY OBSERVATIONS

Date: _____

Adult or kitten: _____

Colour of fur: _____

Colour of eyes: _____

Special physical features:

_____

_____

Behaviour:

_____

_____

Balinese cats do not have a thick undercoat so, like other Asian cats, they like to snuggle up with each other to keep warm. Kittens are usually paler than adults.

# MY DRAWINGS AND PHOTOS

I saw this cat:   in a house ◯   in a garden ◯

# Balinese

When Balinese cats walk, they sweep their long, fluffy tails from side to side. This breed is a longhaired Siamese. Although the fur is long, it is not dense, which gives the cat a dainty appearance and a fine, silky coat. Balinese have inherited some of the Siamese personality, and can be quite demanding although not always as talkative.

**SIZE** Medium

**EYE COLOUR** Blue

**FUR COLOUR** Shades of cream with darker points

**CHARACTER** Playful and good-natured

**SPECIAL FEATURE** Demanding

**COUNTRY OF ORIGIN** USA

Ears may be tufted

Almond-shaped eyes

Long, elegant neck and body

Small paws

Long hind legs

Tufted tail

SEEN IT?

 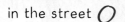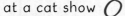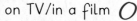

# MY OBSERVATIONS

Date: _____

Adult or kitten: _____

Colour of fur: _____

Colour of eyes: _____

Special physical features:

_____

_____

Behaviour:

_____

_____

_____

Wild cats hunt small animals to eat, so it is no wonder that Highland Lynxes are expert hunters with a strong instinct to seek and catch small prey such as mice and birds.

# MY DRAWINGS AND PHOTOS

I saw this cat:   in a house  ◯    in a garden  ◯

# Highland Lynx

First developed in the USA, the Highland Lynx is a new, rare breed. It was created by breeding a wild Desert Lynx with a Chausie. Highland Lynxes are always active, exploring and playing. They are very friendly, too, and are often said to have dog-like personalities as they are loyal and can be taught tricks.

**SIZE** Large

**EYE COLOUR** Gold, green or blue

**FUR COLOUR** Various colours with a range of tabby patterns

**CHARACTER** Active and energetic

**SPECIAL FEATURE** Many have extra toes

**COUNTRY OF ORIGIN** USA

Large head

Curled ears

Tabby markings

Short tail

Long fur

Strong, muscular body

Paws often have an extra toe

SEEN IT?

# MY OBSERVATIONS

Date:

Adult or kitten:

Colour of fur:

Colour of eyes:

Special physical features:

Behaviour:

All kittens practise stalking and catching prey as soon as they can. This Japanese Bobtail kitten is a bicolour of red and white with tabby stripes on its belly.

# MY DRAWINGS AND PHOTOS

I saw this cat:    in a house  ◯    in a garden  ◯

# Japanese Bobtail

Both longhaired and shorthaired Japanese Bobtails exist. Their coats are silky and smooth, and they are normally tabby or patterned with white. A common colour is black, red and white tortoiseshell (known as three-colour tortie and white). They are named after their short, 'bobbed' tail. These cats are playful, friendly and clever, and have a habit of raising one paw.

SIZE  Small-medium

EYE COLOUR  Any

FUR COLOUR  Various, especially three-colour

CHARACTER  Sociable and talkative

SPECIAL FEATURE  Raises one paw

COUNTRY OF ORIGIN  USA

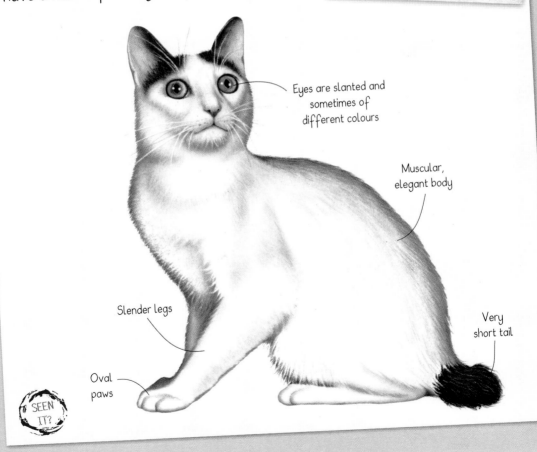

Eyes are slanted and sometimes of different colours

Muscular, elegant body

Slender legs

Very short tail

Oval paws

SEEN IT?

# MY OBSERVATIONS

Date: _____

Adult or kitten: _____

Colour of fur: _____

Colour of eyes: _____

Special physical features: _____

_____

_____

Behaviour: _____

_____

_____

## MY DRAWINGS AND PHOTOS

Some LaPerms are born with curly fur that soon falls out. Later, a new, thicker coat of adult fur grows in. Some kittens in a litter may have straight fur, while others have curly fur.

I saw this cat:   in a house ◯   in a garden ◯

# LaPerm

LaPerms are descended from a kitten that was born bald, but then grew curly fur. Kittens born to LaPerm parents may be bald, or have straight fur or curly fur. Some even have curly whiskers and ear hair. LaPerms are clever and playful, and can form strong attachments to their owners. They love being cuddled, and rub faces with people they like.

**SIZE** Small-medium

**EYE COLOUR** Any

**FUR COLOUR** Any

**CHARACTER** Curious and demanding

**SPECIAL FEATURE** Curly fur

**COUNTRY OF ORIGIN** USA

Long, slender tail

Wavy fur

Almond-shaped eyes

Long neck

Strong, heavy body

Round paws

SEEN IT?

# MY OBSERVATIONS

Date: _____

Adult or kitten: _____

Colour of fur: _____

Colour of eyes: _____

Special physical features: _____

_____

_____

Behaviour: _____

_____

_____

Manx cats enjoy the outdoor life. They are excellent hunters and were once popular on board ships, where they killed pests such as rats. Farmers also keep them to control mice.

MY DRAWINGS AND PHOTOS

I saw this cat:    in a house  $O$    in a garden  $O$

# Manx

These Shorthairs are peculiar because they lack tails. They developed on the Isle of Man, an island off the west coast of England. Some kittens are born with tail stumps, and Manxes are also known as Risers (tail-less), Stumpies, Stubbies or Longies. Manxes are energetic cats that enjoy climbing, chasing and playing with toys. Longhaired Manxes are called Cymrics.

**SIZE** Medium

**EYE COLOUR** Various

**FUR COLOUR** Various

**CHARACTER** Good-natured and friendly

**SPECIAL FEATURE** Tail-less

**COUNTRY OF ORIGIN** Isle of Man, UK

Strong, stocky body

Round, wide head

Wide ears with slightly rounded tips

No tail

Hind legs are longer than the forelegs

Large paws

SEEN IT?

# MY OBSERVATIONS

Date: _____

Adult or kitten: _____

Colour of fur: _____

Colour of eyes: _____

Special physical features: _____

_____

_____

Behaviour: _____

_____

_____

Although Norwegian Forest cats are large, with plenty of fur, they have quite delicate heads with very attractive faces. This is a sturdy, muscular breed with few health problems.

# MY DRAWINGS AND PHOTOS

I saw this cat:   in a house  $O$    in a garden  $O$

# Norwegian Forest

This is an old breed from Norway – a cold country where an extra-thick undercoat is essential for an outdoor cat. Norwegian Forests, or 'weegies' as they are sometimes called, can cope with very cold weather and their fur dries quickly if it gets wet. They are clever cats that enjoy hunting and climbing, and will even investigate running water, looking for fish to catch. Their temperament is playful and loving.

**SIZE** Large

**EYE COLOUR** Any

**FUR COLOUR** All colours and patterns

**CHARACTER** Tough and adventurous

**SPECIAL FEATURE** Quick-drying fur

**COUNTRY OF ORIGIN** Norway

Long hair in ears

Triangular-shaped face

Large, oval eyes

Fur around neck, chest and legs is long and fluffy

Woolly undercoat is covered by longer top coat

Fluffy tail

SEEN IT?

# MY OBSERVATIONS

Date:

Adult or kitten:

Colour of fur:

Colour of eyes:

Special physical features:

Behaviour:

This spotted Ocicat has the athletic body that is typical of the breed. Ocicat owners often describe their pets as being dog-like, as they are loyal and often follow people around.

## MY DRAWINGS AND PHOTOS

I saw this cat:    in a house  ⭕    in a garden  ⭕

# Ocicat

Ocicats look like the wild cats, ocelots; hence their name. However, they are not bred from wild cats, but from Siamese, Abyssinians and American Shorthairs. They have the beautiful markings of wild cats, but have a sweet, tame nature. They are energetic, adore company and can be bossy towards other cats. Ocicats can live for 18 years or more.

SIZE  Medium-large

EYE COLOUR  All

FUR COLOUR  Various, with spots, tabby markings and dark tips to some hairs

CHARACTER  Sociable and lively

SPECIAL FEATURE  Long-lived

COUNTRY OF ORIGIN  USA

Long tail

Arched neck

Long face

Heavy, graceful body

Deep chin

Muscled legs

Oval paws

SEEN IT?

# MY OBSERVATIONS

Date: _____

Adult or kitten: _____

Colour of fur: _____

Colour of eyes: _____

Special physical features: _____

_____

_____

Behaviour: _____

_____

_____

This Pixie-bob is being checked by a judge at a cat show. The paws are so big because these cats have extra toes – a condition called 'polydactyl' and is common in Pixie-bobs.

## MY DRAWINGS AND PHOTOS

I saw this cat:  in a house  ⬭  in a garden  ⬭

# Pixie-bob

A new breed, the Pixie-bob has only been around since the 1980s. Although they resemble wild bobcats, Pixie-bobs are actually descended from domestic cats with spots and short tails. It takes these cats about three years to reach adulthood, whereas most cats mature in just one year. They rarely miaow, but like to chat with other cats and their owners by purring and chirping.

**SIZE** Large

**EYE COLOUR** Gold or gold with hazel flecks

**FUR COLOUR** Shades of brown with markings

**CHARACTER** Loyal and bold

**SPECIAL FEATURE** Short tail

**COUNTRY OF ORIGIN** USA

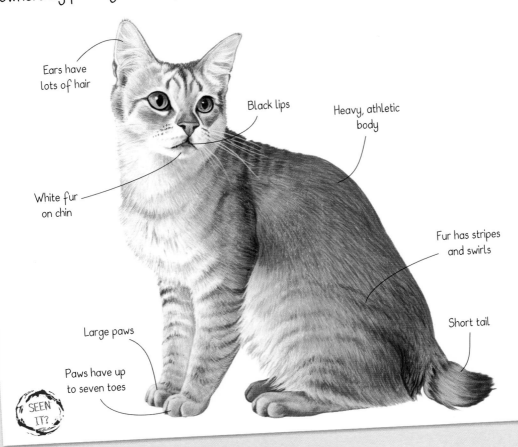

Ears have lots of hair

Black lips

Heavy, athletic body

White fur on chin

Fur has stripes and swirls

Large paws

Paws have up to seven toes

Short tail

SEEN IT?

in the street  O    at a cat show  O    on TV/in a film  O

# MY OBSERVATIONS

Date:

Adult or kitten:

Colour of fur:

Colour of eyes:

Special physical features:



Behaviour:



It is essential that Ragdoll cats are groomed regularly from an early age so they become used to it. Without this attention, their long fur can get matted and dirty.

## MY DRAWINGS AND PHOTOS

I saw this cat:     in a house  $O$     in a garden  $O$

# Ragdoll

It is thought that Ragdolls are descended from a mixture of Birman and Persian Longhairs. They are unique cats because, when picked up, they relax their bodies and become floppy, just like a ragdoll. Their coats are usually pale, with darker points on the face, ears and paws. Some Ragdolls have white patches, too. They have sweet personalities and enjoy receiving lots of attention.

SIZE  Large

EYE COLOUR  Blue

FUR COLOUR  Various colours with patterns

CHARACTER  Trusting and affectionate

SPECIAL FEATURE  Floppy body

COUNTRY OF ORIGIN  USA

Broad head with a flat top

Large cheeks

Long, heavy-set body

Short neck

Long, bushy tail

SEEN IT?

# MY OBSERVATIONS

Date: _____

Adult or kitten: _____

Colour of fur: _____

Colour of eyes: _____

Special physical features: _____

_____

_____

Behaviour: _____

_____

_____

Sphynxes often have a worried expression because they have such wrinkly faces. With their bendy bodies, these cats can reach most parts of their bodies to lick or scratch themselves.

## MY DRAWINGS AND PHOTOS

I saw this cat:   in a house $O$   in a garden $O$

# Sphynx

Although Sphynxes are famous for being bald, they usually have a fine layer of soft fur, or down. Their skin is warm and soft, and they do not sweat when they get hot. Sphynxes benefit from being washed regularly, and they should be in the shade to prevent sunburn. In winter, they mostly stay indoors to keep warm. They are cuddly and affectionate.

**SIZE** Medium

**EYE COLOUR** Any

**FUR COLOUR** Any

**CHARACTER** Bright and friendly

**SPECIAL FEATURE** Lacks a proper coat of fur

**COUNTRY OF ORIGIN** Canada

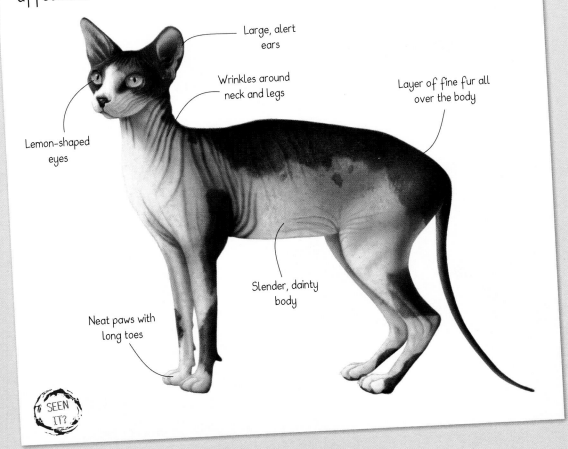

Large, alert ears

Wrinkles around neck and legs

Layer of fine fur all over the body

Lemon-shaped eyes

Slender, dainty body

Neat paws with long toes

SEEN IT?

# Glossary

**Blue** A deep grey shade of fur that appears almost blue.

**Breed** All the cats that share a very similar appearance and personality.

**Breeder** A person who keeps animals to breed them, often to show in competitions or to sell.

**Dense** Fur that is formed when many strands of hair grow from a small area of skin. Dense fur is especially warm.

**Domestic** A cat that lives as a pet, rather than living wild.

**Flecked** A strand of hair that has more than one colour on it.

**Groom** To brush or clean an animal's fur.

**Lilac** A grey shade of fur with a pink tinge.

**Mackerel** A fur pattern that has prominent stripes.

**Marbling** A fur pattern that has streaks of a different colour.

**Muzzle** The nose and mouth of an animal.

**Pedigree** An animal that is a fine example of its breed. Pedigrees may be entered into competitions, and used to breed similar kittens.

**Points** The muzzle, paws, ear tips and tail tip of a cat may be darker in colour than the rest of its fur, and are called its 'points'.

**Purr** The raspy sound a cat makes in its throat when it is contented.

**Red** The colour of fur that is actually more like a pale orange than a red. Red markings often appear on a cream base.

**Seal** A colour of fur that is very dark brown – almost black.

**Tipped** Strands of hair that have dark tips.

**Tortoiseshell** Fur that is made up of hair with two different colours that appear in an irregular way all over the body. The result is a mottled brown that is also described as 'tortie'.

**Undercoat** A layer of dense fur that grows close to a cat's body and keeps it warm.